FUN FACTS

Ripley's

Believe It or Not!®

Kids

& SILLY STORIES 2

PUBLISHING

Consultant Camilla de la Bedoyere
Design Rocket Design
Reprographics Juice Creative

ISBN 978-1-60991-082-2

For information regarding permission, write to
VP Intellectual Property
Ripley Entertainment Inc.
Suite 188, 7576 Kingspointe Parkway
Orlando, Florida 32819

Email: publishing@ripleys.com

Manufactured in China
in June/2013 by Hung Hing
1st printing

Library of Congress Cataloging-in-Publication Data
is available.

PUBLISHER'S NOTE
While every effort has been made to verify the accuracy
of the entries in this book, the Publishers cannot be held
responsible for any errors contained in the work. They
would be glad to receive any information from readers.

WARNING
Some of the stunts and activities in this book are
undertaken by experts and should not be attempted by
anyone without adequate training and supervision.

PUBLISHING

a Jim Pattison Company

FUN FACTS

RiPLeY'S

Believe It or Not!®

KidS

& SILLY STORIES

2

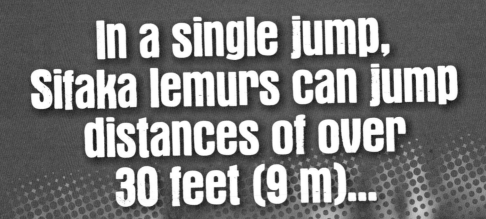

In a single jump, Sifaka lemurs can jump distances of over 30 feet (9 m)...

4

...Believe it or not!

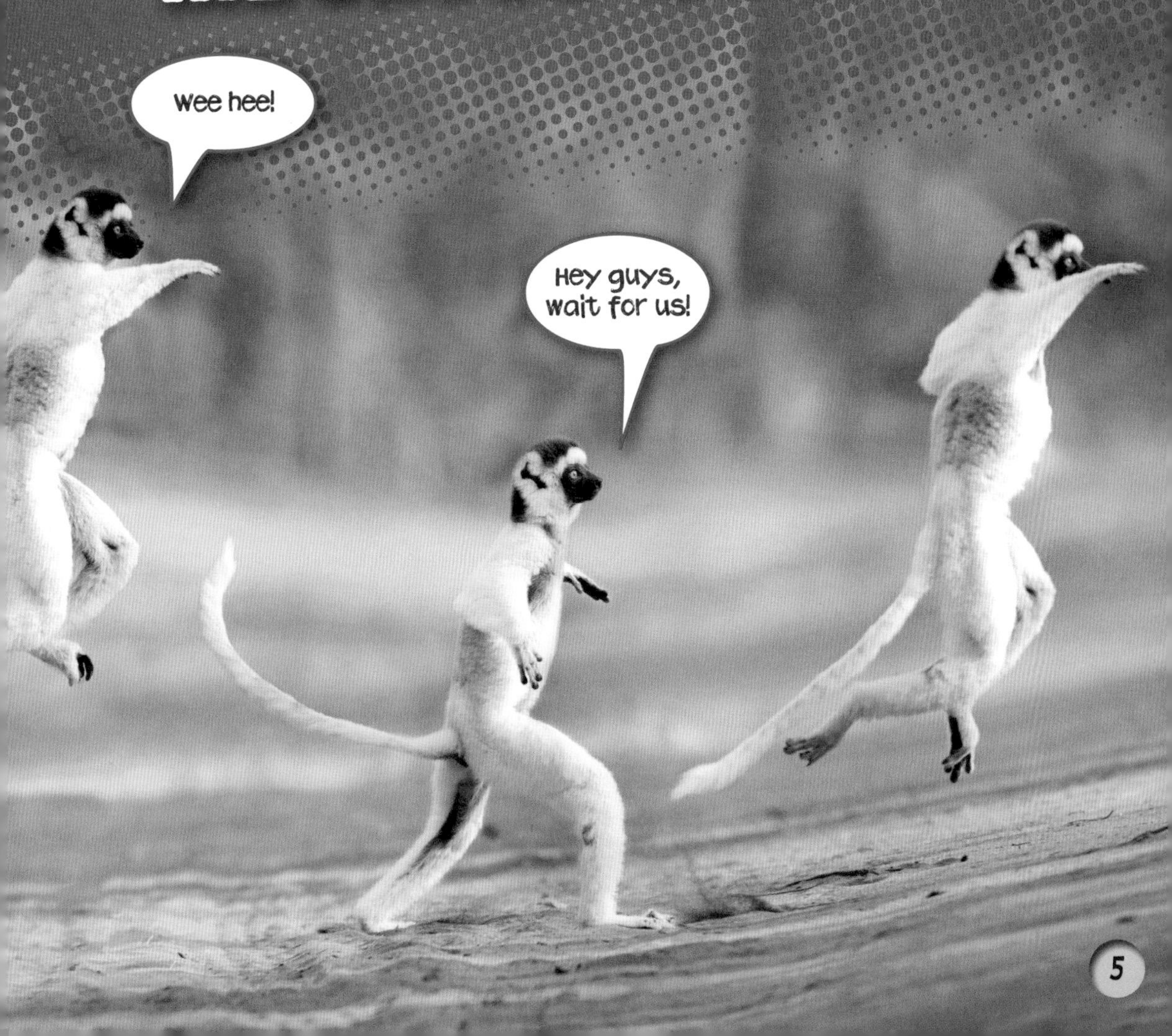

Little Wonders

Willard Wigan's sculptures are so tiny he uses a hair from a fly as a paintbrush!

He once made Alice in Wonderland and breathed her in by mistake!

Beauty and the Beast on a pinhead

Bart and Homer Simpson on a pinhead

Santa Claus in the eye of a needle

A tiny blob of honey fixes the sculptures in the eye of a needle or on top of a pin.

Some frogs FREEZE during winter then UNFREEZE in summer!

Wood frogs have antifreeze-like blood so they can freeze and then thaw with their surroundings.

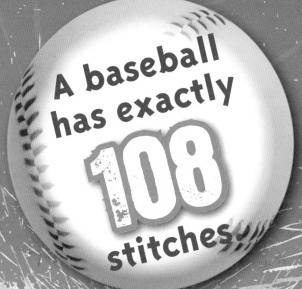

A baseball has exactly 108 stitches.

LOOKING GOOD!

Jane's new seaweed shampoo wasn't what she expected...

Snorkel.. ☑

Mask...... ☑

A stinking, muddy trench.... ☑

At the World Bog Snorkeling Championships in the UK, competitors jump into trenches full of mud wearing snorkels and flippers. They then wade through the course without using swimming strokes, and the fastest through the sludge wins!

111,111,111 × 111,111,111 =

12,345,678,987,654,321

IT'S TRIPLETS!

This is what happens when bananas go **bananas!**

A man in China peeled this banana and found three inside.

Grapes EXPLODE if you microwave them

An average woman wearing lipstick will manage to lick off and eat

one whole lipstick

in her lifetime.

How cool is this?

British artist Lauren Porter knitted a life-size Ferrari!

She used 12 miles (19 km) of wool!

Killer whales breathe together.

When swimming in a group, they all rise to the surface at the same time.

Everyday the world's population flushes away 27,000 trees-worth of toilet paper.

SPLASH DOWN

Professor Splash dives from a height of 35 feet (10.6 m) into a pool just 12 inches (30 cm) deep!

There are mice on Mercury!

Not really, but don't these craters on planet Mercury look like Mickey Mouse's face?!

Astronauts can't cry properly in space because there's no gravity to make tears fall.

If you could smell in space, you might find it smells like a gas station or a barbecue.

OUCH!

One of the world's most poisonous mammals is the

DUCK-BILLED PLATYPUS!

It has a spike on its back leg that injects venom and causes extreme pain.

La, la la la la la laaaa!

Some male mice sing to attract mates.

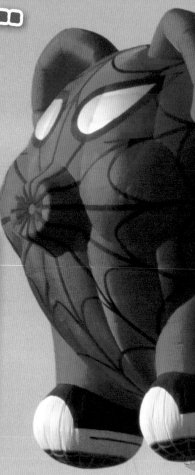

and candy and motorcycles too... in these wacky hot-air balloons.

A piece of paper CAN be folded in half more than EIGHT times!

In fact, the record for folding a piece of paper in half is 13 times!

There are **842** separate languages in Papua New Guinea.

A South Korean grandmother failed 949 written tests before getting her driver's license.

Then she had to pass the practical exam!

Check out the European Beard and Moustache Championships in France. Which one do you like best?

NATURE'S FACES

Crazy plant roots!

Why the long face?

Watch it petal!

Freaky faces turn up in the most unexpected places.

33

CIRCLE OF LIFE

Baby giraffes fall six feet when they are born!

OUCH!

If you yelled for one year, seven months, 26 days, 26 minutes, and 40 seconds you would make enough sound energy to heat one cup of coffee.

Australia has 23 million people and 120 million sheep!

MIGHTY MITE

Ants can lift objects that are fifty times their bodyweight. That's the same as you being able to lift a small car!

There are no ants in Antarctica.

FIRE ANTS

CAN SWITCH OFF TRAFFIC LIGHTS!

THEY LOVE CHEWING THROUGH ELECTRIC WIRE SO MUCH THAT THEY ONCE MANAGED TO SWITCH THEM OFF.

WHO GOES THERE?

Can you
tell who these
animal eyes
belong to?

A group of kangaroos

is called a MOB

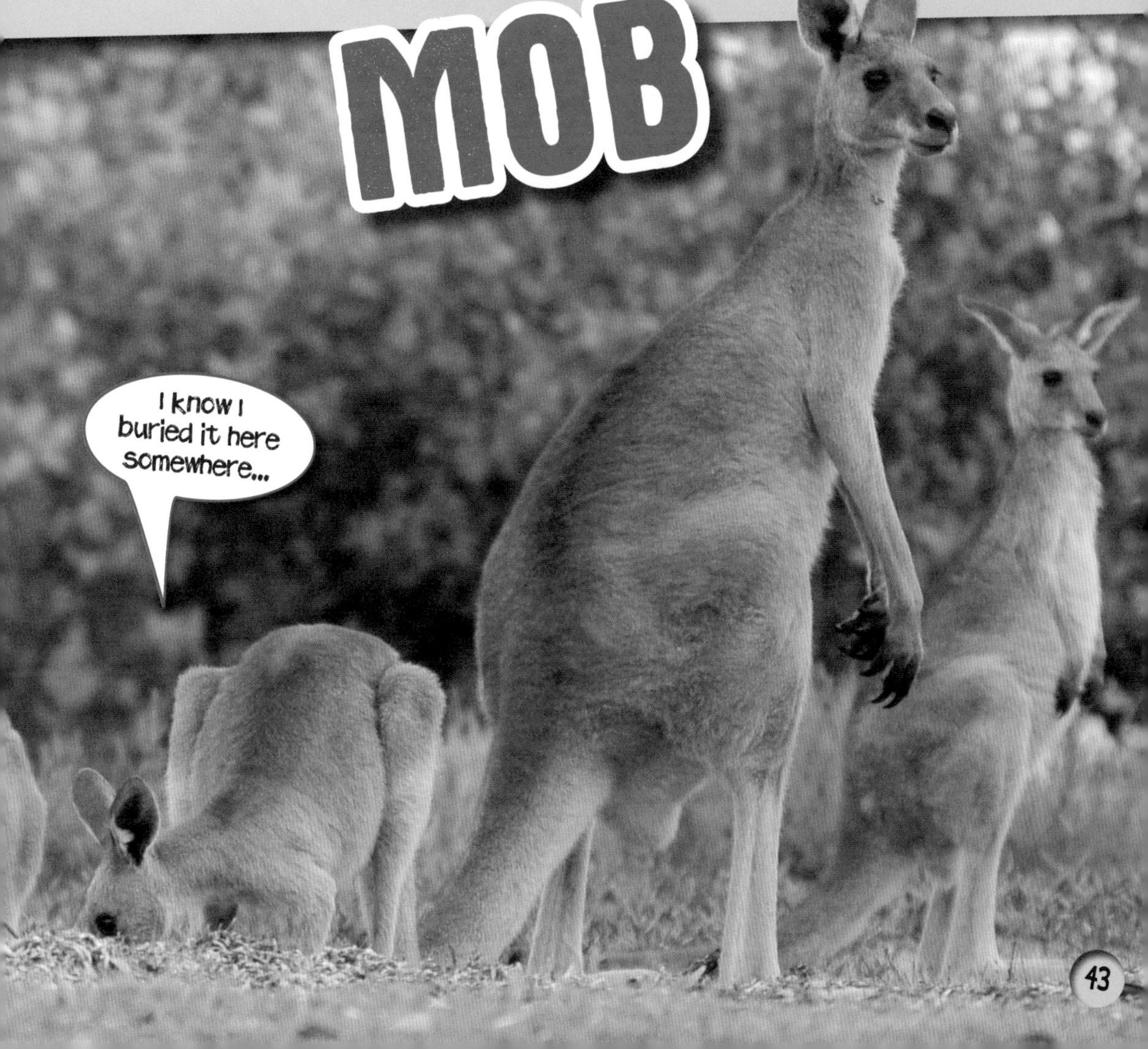

A Waldo get-together in Ireland in 2011. There are 3,657 of them!

Flies taste with their legs.

Do they have cheesy feet?

A blue whale's tongue weighs more than an elephant.

Aaaaargh!

Geniophobia is a fear of CHINS.

An inflatable monkey was covered with 10,000 flip-flops in a park in Brazil by Dutch artist Florentijn Hofman.

2,893,500

of the cells in your body will die and be replaced with new cells in the time it takes you to read this line.

About

5,000

of them would fit on the period at the end of this sentence.

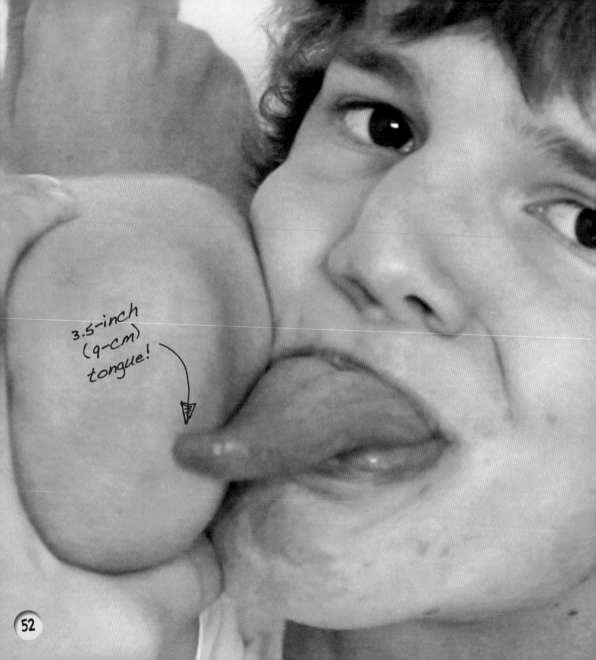

3.5-inch
(9-cm)
tongue!

Can you lick your elbow? Try it!

Most people can't. However, Nick Afanasiev can lick his elbow easily because he has a really long tongue!

Smiling takes one more muscle than frowning.

FEELING DRAINED

Stop the traffic!

A squirrel popped his head up through a drain cover in the middle of a busy road—and got stuck!

Rescuers soaked the squirrel in olive oil until he was slippery enough to slide out.

A BANANA SKIN WILL SHINE YOUR SHOES.

Trapped Wind

Boing!!

Wolfe Bowart from Australia spends his life popping in and out of balloons!

LAZY LIONS

Lions rest for up to 20 hours a day.

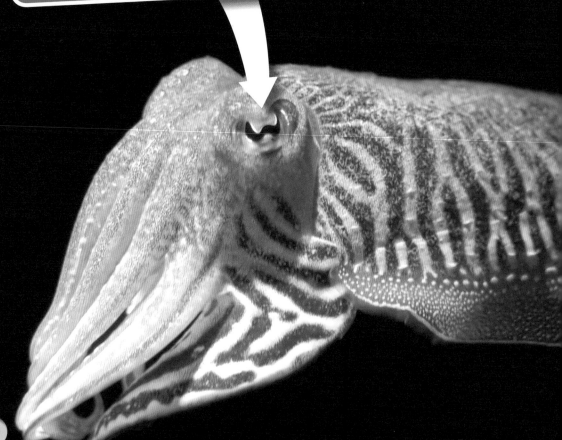

The dot over the letter "i" is called a TITTLE.

PIRATES BELIEVED EARRINGS IMPROVED THEIR EYESIGHT.

Land ahoy!

Where? ...hang on, I can't see a thing without my earrings.

Gary Craig pulled on 302 pairs of underpants in 2012.

There are 43,252,003,274,489,856,000 possible patterns you can make with a Rubik's Cube.

Your stomach grows a new lining every three to seven **days.**

Quick, take it off John, the cops are coming!

It is against the law for a driver to be blindfolded while driving a car in Alabama.

A leech has two brains.

I'm still a low-down, dirty blood sucker!

Arachibutyrophobia

is the fear of peanut butter sticking to the roof of the mouth.

It takes about 540 peanuts to make a small jar of peanut butter.

The average American kid will eat around 1,500 peanut butter sandwiches by the end of high school.

WORLD'S SMALLEST PAIR OF SHOES

Each shoe measures 0.15 inches (3.8 mm) long, 0.7 inches (1.8 mm) wide and 0.9 inches (2.2 mm) high.

In Kentucky, it is illegal to carry an ICE CREAM CONE in your pocket.

When you **sneeze**, germs and dirt fly out of your nose at **35 mph** (56 km/h).

Drinking too much water can kill you.

Wolf eels are called the UGLY old men of the sea.

But not to their face—their bite is strong enough to crush crabs!

We may be ugly, but we've got each other.

WIGGLY TONGUES

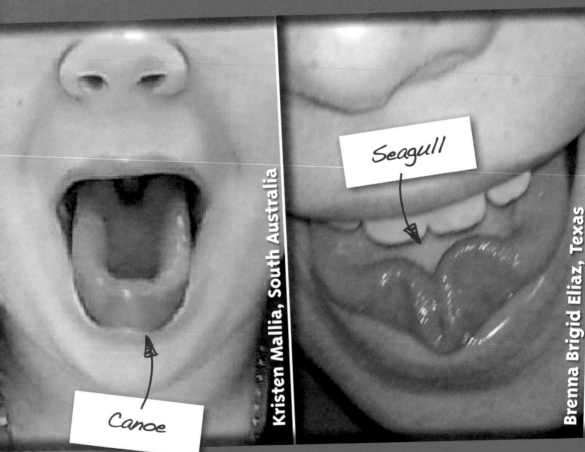

Canoe

Kristen Mallia, South Australia

Seagull

Brenna Brigid Eliaz, Texas

Readers sent us pictures of the crazy tongue shapes they can make.

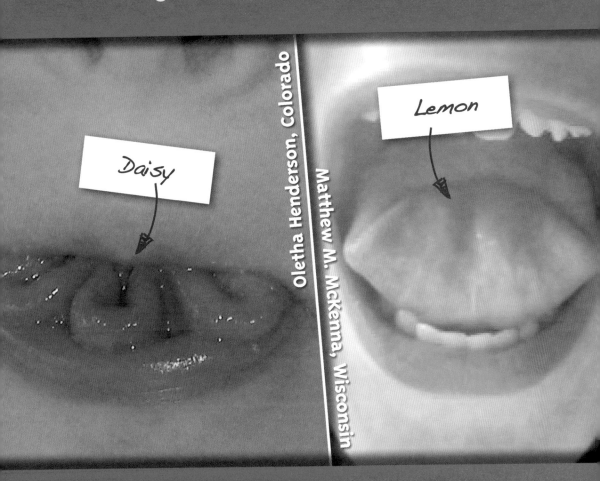

Daisy

Oletha Henderson, Colorado

Lemon

Matthew M. McKenna, Wisconsin

And they're off!

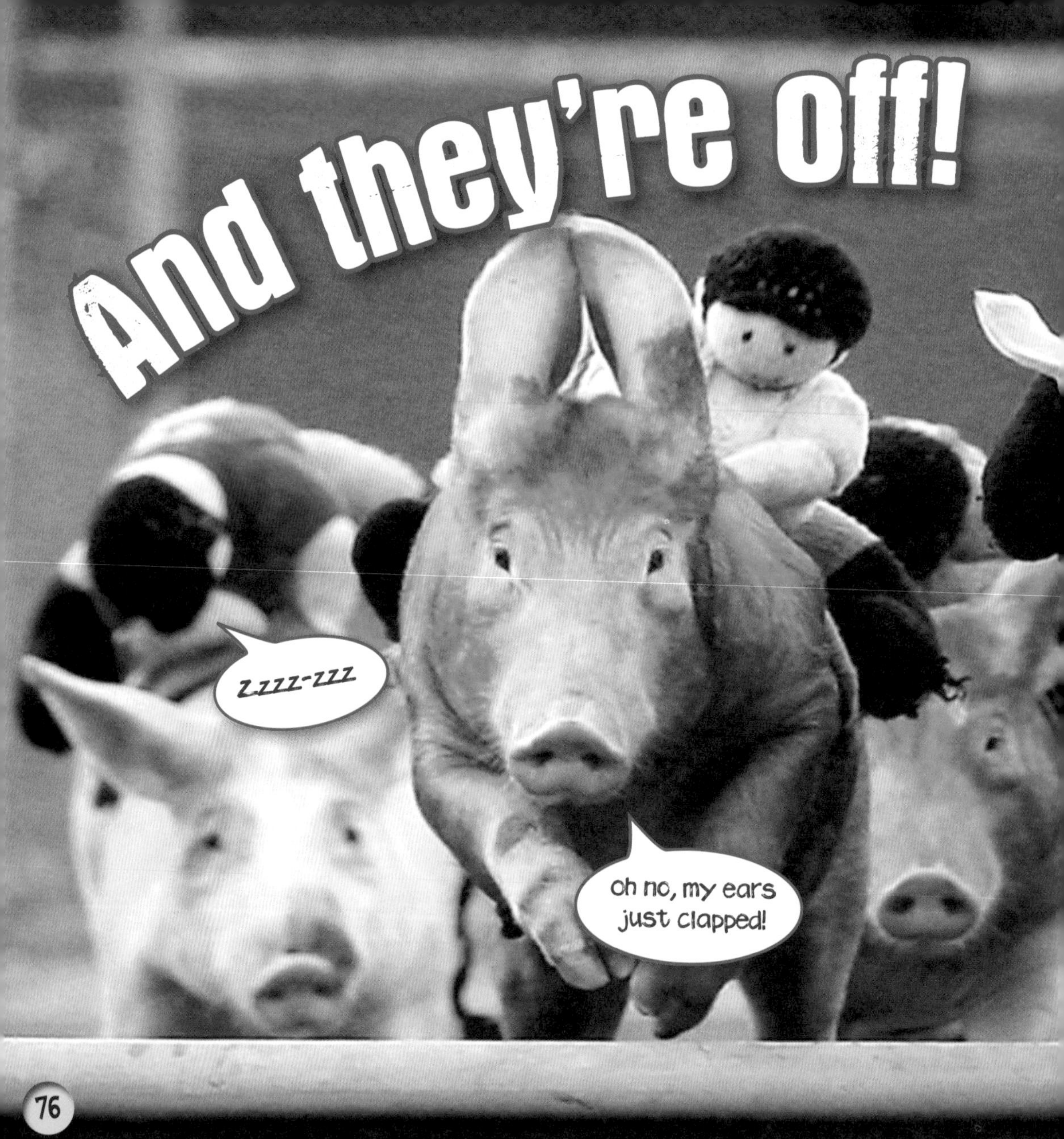

Up, Up and Away

Kayleigh O'Connor loves the film *Up* so much that she's decorated her nails with a whole scene from it. On her thumb, a house floats from a bunch of balloons. Her fingernails resemble sky, complete with fluffy clouds.

An average pencil will write about 50,000 words before running out.

Baby octopuses are about the size of a flea when they are born.

13,400 Pokémon... and counting!

CRAZY ABOUT POKÉMON

Lisa Courtney has more Pokémon than anyone else in the world!

They've taken over her home in England. She's so obsessed that she regularly travels to Japan, where the video-game character was created, to collect the latest models.

Do polar bears dance?

No... this one was trying very hard to stand up and was just a bit wobbly rather than groovy!

AIR-JACKED

Take me to the seaside... NOW!

Believe it or not, this eagle was attacked by a seagull!

Crayfish have teeth in their stomachs and kidneys in their heads.

A **BLINK** LASTS ABOUT 0.3 SECONDS.

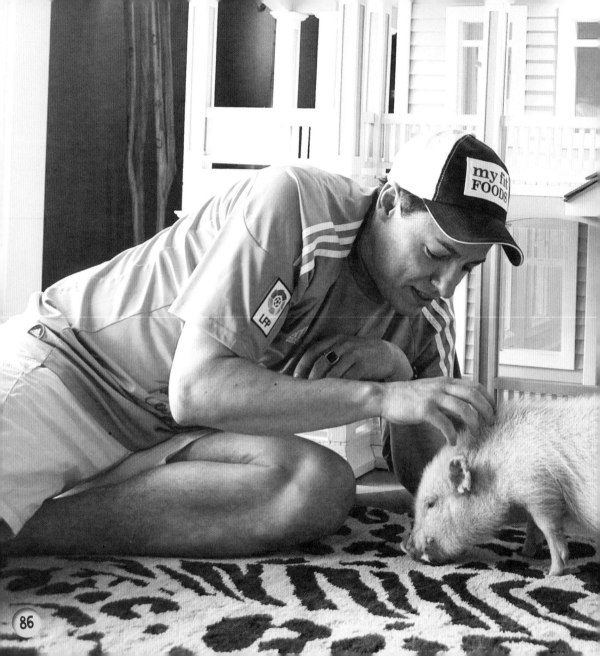

Pig Sty-le

Guillermo Gonzales loves his piglets so much he had a miniature replica of his house made for them and put it in his living room, in Austin, Texas.

I'll put the trash out dear.

AND THE WINNER IS...

the first person to eat a pie without using their hands!

Guzzle

This pie-eating contest took place in Los Angeles.

Nicholas Peake, a teacher from England, has been coughing up to **100 times an hour for 15 years!**

20 volcanoes are erupting right now!

MUTANT KILLER PENGUINS!

Penguins can bend their heads all the way back to scratch their own backs! They have double-jointed necks, which help them get to any hard to reach places.

wooooo!

John Coker's hobby is building rockets. He designed eight as a giant box of crayons and, after six years of planning, took them to the Nevada Desert to set them off.

Only four crayons flew, but they reached 2,928 feet (892 m).

Crayola
ROCKETS
8

21

This number, with 100 zeros, is called a googol.

10,000,000,000,000,000,000,000,000,
000,000,000,000,000,000,000,000,00
0,000,000,000,000,000,000,000,000,
000,000,000,000,000,000,000,000

The Internet search engine Google takes its name from the crazy huge number "googol." It was chosen because of the huge amount of information on the web.

CUBISM

This portrait of SpongeBob SquarePants is made out of 150 Rubik's Cubes. Josh Chalom needed 30 helpers to twist Rubik's Cubes to show the correct patterns for the picture.

A frog has to blink to swallow!

Blinking pushes its eyeballs down on top of its mouth and pushes food down its throat.

Your body produces half a gallon of gas each day in BURPS AND FARTS!

Pharp...

oh dear, pardon me!

THERE'S A TOWN IN NORWAY CALLED "HELL"

OWLS HAVE 3 EYELIDS

FOWL PLAY

Jim?

No, it's Dave

Whose smart idea was this?

A Chinese farmer came up with special glasses for his chickens to stop them fighting. The glasses stop the chickens looking straight ahead—and now they don't fight.

BEST HOOF FORWARD

Sprout, a miniature horse from Colorado Springs, wears shoes!

The tiny horse volunteers at the local hospital—bringing a smile to people's faces—but after falling over on the slippery floor, his owner, Gretchen Long, tried some teddy bear sneakers for size. Now, he can trot around the hospital without a stumble!

SOME CLOUDS WEIGH AS MUCH AS 85 ELEPHANTS!

In China, fish and chips are served with sugar.

yuk!

Tasty Face

Every day for a **whole year** American artist James Kuhn painted his face with a different design.

Some of his designs were food themed, such as these burger, popcorn, and pineapple faces.

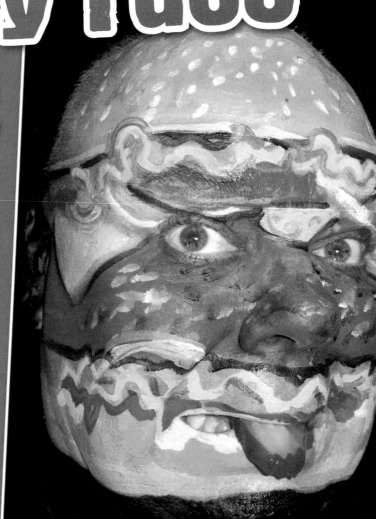

SPIDER SNACK

- Take one black tarantula.

- Fry in hot oil with salt and sugar.

- Top with wafer-thin garlic slices.

- Serve as a snack in Cambodia.

Eeww, GROSS!

COWS HAVE ACCENTS

Farmers in England have said that their cows have different moos depending on which herd they come from.

cor blimey Guv!

PRETTY POOL

Lake Hillier in Western Australia is pink and no one knows why.

Even when the water is taken away in a container, it's still pink!

There are two golf balls sitting on the Moon.

They were hit by American astronaut Alan Shepard when he walked on the Moon in 1971.

It's a Whopper!

There are ten fields of these giant mushrooms in China.

When farmer Rong Guiling bought the seeds, she was told the mushrooms would be small white ones!

Plant-eating insects' poop is called frass.

In under one minute, your heart pumps blood to every cell in your body.

A tick eats just **3** times in its life.

Cockroaches can live for a month without food.

Do unicorns exist?

Massive? How rude, it's distinguished.

No, but there are unicorn fish. They have a massive horn at the front of their head.

SPLOOOOSH!

Erghh, that's gonna whiff!

"Milking" is the new craze in the U.K.

Take one four-pint container of milk.
Stand in a public place.
Pour milk over head.
Take a video and post on YouTube.

You share your birthday with at least

19 million other people.

CREEPY CRAWLEY

Do caterpillars celebrate Halloween?

No, but the pink underwing caterpillar does look like he's wearing a skull mask!

Trick or treat?

The fear of
Halloween
is called
Samhainophobia.

Horned lizards squirt blood from their eyes. They do it to defend themselves.

Wow! 10 feet
(3 m) high.

BIG DADDY

Bigfoot 5 has the largest Monster Truck wheels ever!

SWEET DREAMS

Seven pandas were born within three months of each other in a sanctuary in China in 2012. They got to have a sleepover!

A cow can drink a

bathtub

# of water in one day.

Each inch of a human armpit has just over half a million bacteria.

Euwww!

Barking MAD!

What's doga? It's yoga for dogs and their owners, of course! Classes take place in Crystal Beach, Florida.

I'd rather chase a stick in the park!

Take cover!

The heart pumps blood around the body so hard it could squirt it 30 feet (9 m) across the room.

A book borrowed from Sidney Sussex College, England, was finally returned 288 years later.

COW GIRL

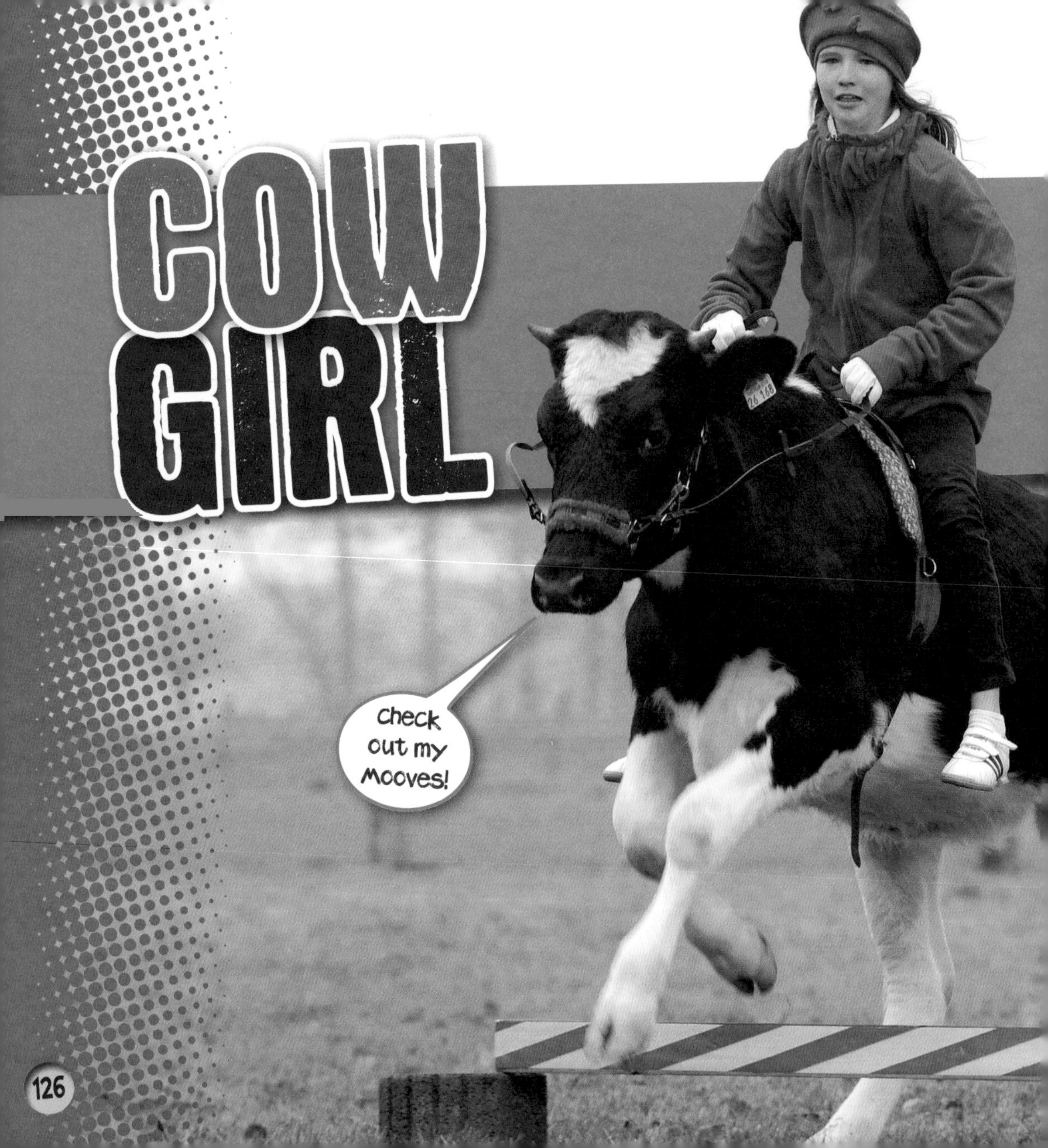

When her parents said no to a horse, Iris Becker learned how to ride a cow.

Americans Brian and Steve Seibel played table tennis without stopping for 8 hours 15 minutes and 1 second in 2004.

They hold the world record for hitting the ball back and forth to each other without dropping it or stopping.

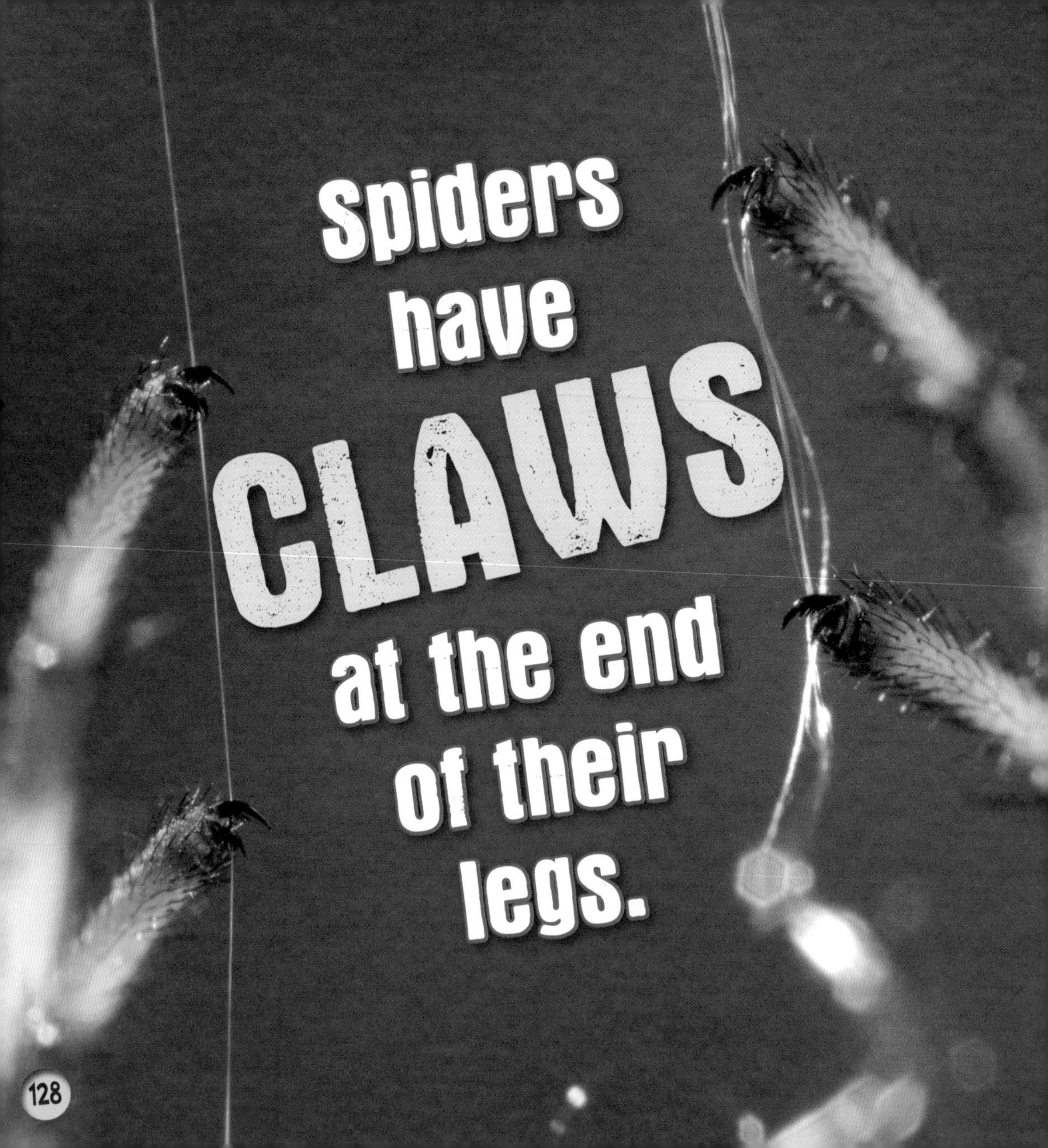

Spiders
have
CLAWS
at the end
of their
legs.

Barbie dolls in Japan are now made with their lips closed and have no teeth.

BALL BOY

It took Joel Waul five years to make the biggest rubber band ball in the world!

9,432 pounds (4,282 kg)

7 feet tall (2.1 m)

130

HOT water freezes faster than COLD water.

Your fingernails take about six months to grow from the base to the tip.

What a Yarn!

It took 4 million stitches and 50 miles (80 km) of wool to create this life-size knitted garden.

Golden Grin

Sebastian, a black Persian cat, has two gold crowns on his bottom teeth.

Now you die... Mr Bond!

His teeth stuck out, so the crowns were added for strength.

A clam taken from the sea north of Iceland was

405 years old!

There is a breed of dog with TWO noses!

The double-nosed Andean tiger hound is a hunting dog with an excellent sense of smell.

An **eyelash** lasts for approximately 75 days before falling out.

Some bamboo plants grow **3 feet** (0.9 m) in 24 hours.

An earthworm found in South Africa measured 22 feet long.

(6.7 m).

WOW!

DOGS DRIVE CARS!

Yes, they really do!
In New Zealand, dogs
are being taught to
drive cars to prove
how clever they are.
Monty, Ginny, and
Porter learned how to
move the gearshift,
accelerator, brake and
steering wheel.

139

How Much?

A woman in Thailand spent

$16,240

on a wedding for her cat.

The body of the average baby is 75% water.

When porcupines are mad they stomp their feet!

oooo... Get you!

The largest spider ever found had a diameter of 17 inches (50 cm). It was the Megarachne from Argentina.

An average person uses the toilet **2,500** times a year.

Roy C. Sullivan, from Virginia, was struck by lightning **seven** times between 1942 and 1977.

FREAKY TEETH

BABIRUSA

Upper canines pierce the skin of its upper jaw and grow through the skull.

Give us a kiss!

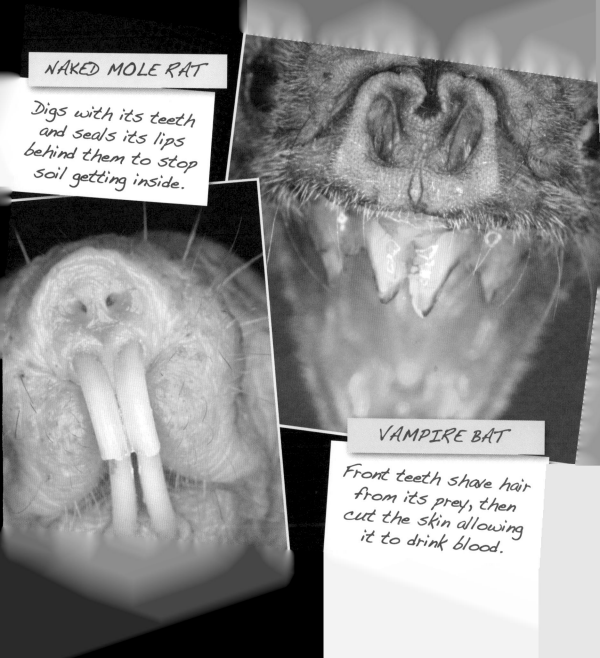

NAKED MOLE RAT

Digs with its teeth and seals its lips behind them to stop soil getting inside.

VAMPIRE BAT

Front teeth shave hair from its prey, then cut the skin allowing it to drink blood.

EGGPLOSION!

Marble traveling at 447 mph (720 km/h)

Look what happens when you fire a marble at an egg and take a picture!

Lemons contain more sugar than strawberries.

Roughly one out of every 55 Canadian women give birth in their car on the way to the hospital.

Just drive Gordon!!

Look, it's a greater spotted warbler!

Pizza Problem?

Breakfast: Pizza
Lunch: Pizza
Dinner: Pizza
Snacks: more Pizza!

Sophie Ray has eaten nothing but plain pizza for the last eight years—even a slice of pepperoni is enough to turn her stomach!

Sticky Pictures

Ben Wilson paints on chewing gum stuck to the streets of London.

Look where you step, I've only just painted that!

There are thousands of the tiny artworks all over the city—you just have to know where to look!

You have a unique tongue print.

Like fingerprints, it can be used for identification.

How did you find the cake thief, Sarge?

The accused left their tongue prints all over it, sir.

One in ten people lives on an island.

There are more plastic flamingos in the United States, than real ones!

ENGLISH

The big breakfast at Jester's Diner, in the U.K., weighs the same as a small child.

So far, no one's finished it!

Papakolea Beach in Hawaii has **green** sand.

Randy Gardner went without sleep for 264 hours 12 minutes in 1964.

Afterward, he slept for just 14 hours 40 minutes.

BATS HAVE THUMBS.

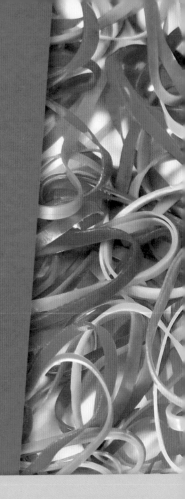

Rubber bands last longer when kept in the fridge.

DELISH-ART

Believe it or not, you can't eat this dinner. It's an oil painting made by Tjalf Sparnaay from the Netherlands.

CHEEKY CHOPS

Hey, watch this.

A chipmunk's cheeks are three times bigger than its head... when stuffed.

LONELY LIFE

An elderly couple in China refused to allow their house to be knocked down... so a new road had to be built around it.

A blue whale makes a noise louder than a jumbo jet.

A crocodile can spend up to an HOUR under water without breathing.

It manages to do this by slowing its heart rate down to two or three beats a minute.

Gasp!

Most people lose between 50 and 100 hairs from their head every day!

Chameleons can look forward and backward at the same time!
Each eye can move independently.

Hey, I've got my eye on you...

...and you!

Joann Osterud flew an
aircraft upside down for
4 hours
38 minutes
10 seconds
over Canada in 1991.

The Hawaiian alphabet has only 12 letters.

Neck Ache!

37.5 inches
(95 cm) long

Lurch, a Watusi bull from Arkansas, had the world's biggest horns.

weighing 100 pounds
(45.4 kg) each

I-DO!

I-FAIRY

You May Now Kiss the Robot...

I-Fairy, a robot, helped out at this wedding in Tokyo, Japan. It was the first wedding in the world to be led by a robot.

The wife of a Sultan is called a Sultana.

It's impossible to tickle yourself. Try it!

One part of your brain warns the rest of your brain that you are about to tickle yourself. Since your brain knows this, it ignores the tickle.

Good job too if you ask me!

Elephants are the only mammals that can't jump.

No words in the dictionary rhyme with orange.

He's NUTS!

Sammy the squirrel spends hours playing the piano!

He lives in England with piano teacher Shirley Higton and started disturbing her lessons by scampering all over the keys. He has now been bought his own instrument.

SUCH FUN!

Derek never takes hunting seriously

The mouth of a hyena is so tough it can chew through a

GLASS BOTTLE

without cutting itself.

After spotted hyenas have caught their prey they celebrate by making a noise that sounds like a

GIGGLE.

This alerts the other hyenas to come and share the food.

HEAD IN THE CLOUDS

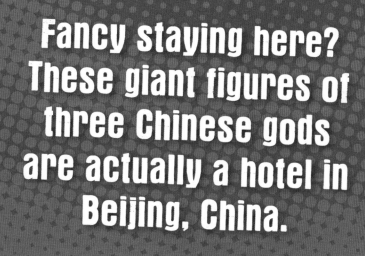

Fancy staying here? These giant figures of three Chinese gods are actually a hotel in Beijing, China.

You Must Be Yoking!

A cook was amazed to crack open seven eggs one after the other and discover they were all double-yolked!

An egg with two yolks is so rare, you might have to crack open a thousand eggs to find one.

SPARKLING RIDE

Ken and Annie Burkitt from Niagara Falls, Canada, decorated their car with crystals showing famous places in America.

Can you spot the Statue of Liberty?

Mini Cooper car covered in more than one million crystals!

Beach Monster

This mighty mosaic dragon on a beach in China is made from 900 tents!

You will produce enough saliva to fill a swimming pool during your lifetime.

Really gross!

A shrew's heart beats **1,000** times a minute...

...but an elephant's beats only around **30** times a minute.

Your brain does not feel pain.

It can send out pain signals to the rest of your body, but the brain itself does not actually feel pain.

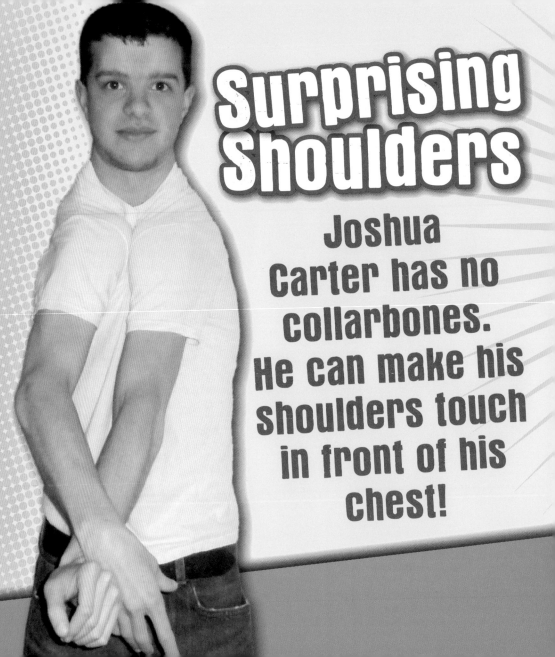

Surprising Shoulders

Joshua Carter has no collarbones. He can make his shoulders touch in front of his chest!

The average ear grows 0.01 inches (0.03 cm) in length every year.

The distance between your elbow and your wrist is the same length as your foot.

In Ancient Rome, bald men often painted hair onto their scalps.

QUIRKY QUARTET

Oleksandr Bozhyk can play four violins at once!

Birds don't sweat.

They have no sweat glands.

3 babies are born in the world every second.

If all strawberries grown in California each year were put side by side, they would wrap around the Earth 15 times.

HOUSE MUSIC

Every time it rains, the pipes that cover this building in Dresden, Germany, become a giant musical instrument and play a tune.

Barry Yip from Hong Kong once spent 81 hours and 23 seconds singing 1,000 karaoke songs.

The chances of giving birth to identical triplets is **1 in 200 million.**

Giraffe hooves are as big as dinner plates.

SKY SURFER

This cloud over England looks more like a dolphin than rain.

Babies don't cry.

They don't shed tears until they are about 8 months old—when their tear ducts are fully developed.

DOZING DRIVER

Masik the squirrel was found abandoned as a baby and was nursed back to health. He is so devoted to the man who found him that he even dozes on the steering wheel while his owner drives!

It is against the law to take a **LION** into a cinema in Baltimore, Maryland.

Aaarghh

Run for your lives!

Honeybees beat their wings about

11,500

times a minute!

Your body sheds around 500,000,000 flakes of skin every day.

Really gross!

This beautiful burger was made by Henry Hargreaves from New York.

Yes, it's edible!

RAINBOW BURGER

- Take two quarter pounders—one yellow, one blue.

- Add orange, green, and scarlet beef slices.

- Include some peacock-blue cheese.

- Add purple lettuce.

- Dribble on purple and orange mayo.

- Squeeze between a sesame bun.

- Enjoy!

208

BUG-POPS

Er, I'm fine thanks.

You can buy lollipops filled with disgusting insects! Edible, a company based in the U.K., created the bug-pops using lots of different insects, including worms, scorpions, and ants.

rminate!

A couple in California dressed up their Christmas tree as a Dalek, the fictional alien in the British TV series *Dr Who*.

SEEING RED

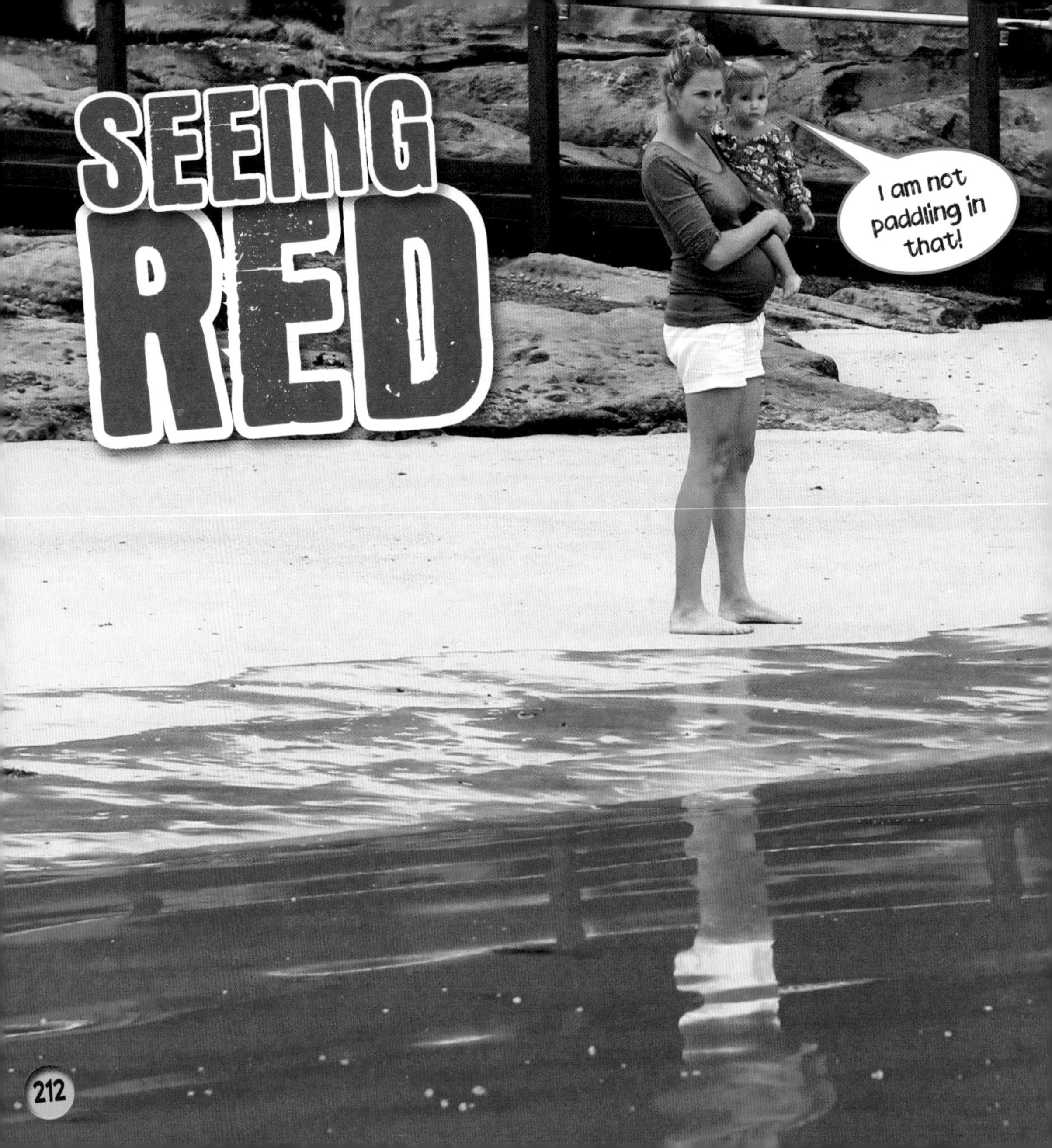

The sea turned red in 2012 at Clovelly Beach, Sydney, Australia.

The blood red water was caused by algae (tiny plants) growing in the sea.

The world's biggest snowflake was 15 inches (38 cm) wide and 8 inches (20 cm) thick. It fell in Montana in the U.S.A. on January 28, 1887.

Take cover!

The human body has about 60,000 miles (97,000 km) of blood vessels.

That's the same distance as 2½ times around the world!

Your nails would grow to about **13 feet** (4 m) long if you never cut them.

You can buy a perfume that smells like cheese.

You smell lovely tonight darling, is it that new "cheese" perfume?

No, it's my feet.

Rugby balls used to be made from pigs' bladders.

You take about 600 million breaths in a lifetime, that's about

23,000

breaths a day!

A bubblegum bubble 20 inches (51 cm) across was blown by Chad Fell from the U.S.A.

Major League baseball teams use about

850,000

balls each season.

Golf balls used to have HONEY in the middle.

Mmm, very tasty!

INDEX

PHOTO CREDITS

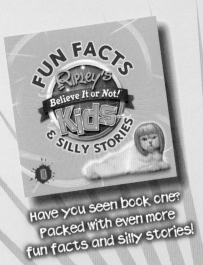
we hope you
enjoyed the book!

If you have a fun fact or silly story, why not
email us at bionresearch@ripleys.com
or write to us at
BION Research, Ripley Entertainment Inc.,
7576 Kingspointe Parkway, 188, Orlando,
Florida 32819, U.S.A.